NEW VANGUARD • 171

MIL MI-24 *HIND* GUNSHIP

ALEXANDER MLADENOV   ILLUSTRATED BY IAN PALMER

First published in Great Britain in 2010 by Osprey Publishing,

Midland House, West Way, Botley, Oxford, OX2 0PH, UK

44–02 23rd St, Suite 219, Long Island City, NY 11101, USA

E-mail: info@ospreypublishing.com

A CIP catalogue record for this book is available from the British Library

Print ISBN: 978 1 84603 953 9

PDF e-book ISBN: 978 1 84603 954 6

Page layout by: Melissa Orrom Swan, Oxford

Index by Mark Parkin

Typeset in Sabon and Myriad Pro

Originated by United Graphics Pte Ltd

Printed in China through World Print Ltd

10 11 12 13 14   10 9 8 7 6 5 4 3 2 1

FOR A CATALOGUE OF ALL BOOKS PUBLISHED BY OSPREY MILITARY AND AVIATION PLEASE CONTACT:

Osprey Direct, c/o Random House Distribution Center,
400 Hahn Road, Westminster, MD 21157
Email: uscustomerservice@ospreypublishing.com

Osprey Direct, The Book Service Ltd, Distribution Centre,
Colchester Road, Frating Green, Colchester, Essex, CO7 7DW
E-mail: customerservice@ospreypublishing.com

www.ospreypublishing.com

Osprey Publishing is supporting the Woodland Trust, the UK's leading woodland conservation charity, by funding the dedication of trees.

EDITOR'S NOTE

For ease of comparison please refer to the following conversion table:

1 mile = 1.6km

1lb = 0.45kg

1yd = 0.9m

1ft = 0.3m

1in = 2.54cm/25.4mm

1gal = 4.5 liters

1 ton (US) = 0.9 tonnes

CONTENTS

MIL MI-24 *HIND* GUNSHIP

INTRODUCTION

The Mi-24 is in a class of its own as a battlefield helicopter and the former Cold War combat aircraft is also the most widely used attack helicopter of all time. Considerably larger and heavier than its conceptual cousin, the Bell AH-1 HueyCobra, the Mi-24 (NATO reporting name *Hind*) was designed in the 1960s as an antitank/close-air-support rotorcraft, and thanks to its large cabin for up to eight fully equipped troops it also has a considerable assault transport capability.

Contrary to the approach to anti-armour helicopter operations taken in the West, which calls for predominantly ambush tactics, the *Hind's* original combat deployment concept – dating from the early to mid-1970s – foresees a deployment much more like a modern-day equivalent of the famous World War II Ilyushin Il-2 *Shturmovik* heavily-armoured low-level attack aircraft. Ingressing in the same large formations and at a slightly lower speed over Cold War-era battlefields in Europe, Mi-24 pilots were taught to employ the same basic tactics as their World War II predecessors flying the *Shturmovik*: approaching the target area at treetop altitude and full speed, popping

A pair of Mi-24PK-2s captured by the camera in a strafing pass – one unleashing S-8 rockets, the other firing the GSh-30K twin-barrelled 30mm gun. (Mil MHP)

out rapidly, mounting a running attack from a shallow dive and then, if threat level permits, circling overhead for additional firing passes.

Today, the aircraft still soldiers on with no fewer than 60 air arms and paramilitary forces around the world. Between late 1969 and late 2009, at least 2,300 examples of all *Hind* variants were produced and at time of writing the *Hind* was still maintained in low-rate production for export customers.

DEVELOPMENT

The idea of introducing into the then Soviet Armed Forces a new class of battlefield helicopters to be used as flying infantry fighting vehicles (IFVs) was born in the early 1960s. The helicopters' main purpose was to deliver troops on the battlefield quickly and precisely and to provide close air support (CAS) to the advancing ground troops, knocking out hardened targets at the forward edge of the battle area. In 1966, the Moscow-based Mil Design Bureau proposed a full-scale mock-up of what its designer-general and founder, Mikhail Leontyevich Mil,

At least 2,300 examples of all Mi-24 derivatives were produced between 1969 and 2009, and the type is offered new in upgraded or "classical" form for export customers. The *Hind* still soldiers on with no fewer than 60 air arms and paramilitary forces around the world. (Alexander Mladenov)

referred to as a rotary-wing IFV. Dubbed V-24, this was a conceptual design only, with both the cockpit and cabin provided with extensive armour protection. At the same time the fuselage was required to be large enough to accommodate a squad of eight fully equipped troops. The armament of the new class of helicopter was to comprise one 23mm gun, rockets and anti-tank guided missiles (ATGMs).

As a conceptual exercise, the V-24's intended role was to stimulate the Soviet military establishment to start thinking about the possible operational use of well-armoured assault and anti-tank helicopters and eventually provide a detailed set of formal requirements for this new class of battlefield rotorcraft. As a direct consequence of this initiative of Mikhail Mil, in 1967 a tender was put out by the Soviet Ministry of Defence, with Mil and Kamov, the two principal helicopter design bureaux in the Soviet Union, competing head-to-head in offering their designs for armoured battlefield helicopters. While Kamov's design teams chose to follow a rather conservative approach by offering a derivative of its Ka-25 multifunctional naval helicopter (designated the Ka-25F), heavily modified for the close air support and assault transport role), Mil's design team ventured to propose a clean sheet design.

In fact, the all-new rotorcraft design proposed by Mil incorporated a good many novelties which had recently been proven on the latest Mi-8 derivatives as well as the new Mi-14 naval helicopter, including the lightweight and powerful Klimov TV3-117 turboshaft engine. Mil also proposed an alternative single-engine configuration with a maximum take-off weight (MTOW) of 15,400lb (7,000kg), while the twin-engine configuration was expected to have an MTOW of 23,100lb (10,500kg). Both the single- and twin-engine configurations featured the same main cabin capable of accommodating up to eight fully-equipped troops.

In the event, Mil's twin-engine design was considered by the Soviet military experts to be far better and more promising than that offered by Kamov, although the Soviet military representatives eventually requested that a plethora of further developments and design alterations be incorporated. They also raised a good many queries and new requirements which the design team had to consider when developing the helicopter. For instance, the Soviet military requested that the 23mm gun be replaced by a flexible 12.7mm machine gun since the ATGMs were viewed as the primary weapons system for knocking out armoured targets. From the very beginning, the new helicopter was earmarked to receive the 9M114 Shturm-V ATGM missile system – then very advanced but still in an early design and development phase – rather than the 9M17P Falanga-V system, readily available at the time but already considered rather outdated and ineffective.

The performance specifications were for a maximum speed of 169–198kt (300–350km/h) and a service ceiling of no less than 9,840ft (3,000m). There were also stringent demands with regard to agility: a maximum g-load in manoeuvring flight of 1.75, with the capability of diving at up to 30 degrees, turning with a bank angle of up to 45 degrees, performing tight U-turns while in climb, and performing many other combat manoeuvres considered useful for attacking ground targets, avoiding ground fire and engaging other helicopters or fixed-wing aircraft.

The design and development phase was formally initiated in accordance with a resolution of the government and the Central Committee of the Communist Party of the Soviet Union dated 6 May 1968. The helicopter was referred to as the V-24 in all government documents though within the Mil Design Bureau the new machine was colloquially known as the Mi-24. The formal internal design bureau designation for the V-24 was *Izdeliye* 240 ("Product 240") and the project was developed under the personal supervision of Mikhail Mil who strictly observed the incorporation of his original "Flying IFV" concept into the V-24's design.

The work on the new rotorcraft advanced rapidly thanks to the use of a good many off-the-shelf parts and assemblies that had already proved themselves on other Mil helicopter designs. The main rotor hub, main and tail rotor blades, swash-plate assembly and transmission components were all borrowed from the Mi-8 and Mi-14 while the highly promising Klimov TV3-117 turboshaft was already flight-tested onboard the Mi-14.

The V-24 introduced an all-new streamlined fuselage featuring a large enclosed cockpit with side-by-side seating for the pilot and weapons-system operator (WSO) behind flat-panel glazing. Initially, the anti-tank guided missiles were intended to be carried on launch rails attached directly onto the fuselage while the unguided weapons were to be suspended on pylons under large stub wings. The design also intended for the stub wings to generate a good deal of lift in high-speed flight, contributing up to 20 per cent of the total lift generated by the rotor-system/stub-wings combination. Fuel was carried in five self-sealing tanks with a total capacity of 1,130 litres (469 Imp gal), and two auxiliary tanks with a total capacity of 1,630 litres (359 Imp gal) can be installed in the cabin if required for long-range flights.

The V-24 was developed in competition with the Kamov Ka-25F, a coaxial attack helicopter to be derived from the Ka-25 shipborne submarine hunter. In the event the Ka-25F remained only as a deck-size mock-up. (OAO Kamov, via Alexander Mladenov)

The V-24 design was finalised in February 1969 and final assembly of the first prototype commenced shortly afterwards. This was rolled out of the assembly hall at Mil's experimental plant at Panki, near Moscow, and made its maiden hovering flight in the capable hands of Mil test pilot German Alferov on 19 September 1969.

Sadly, the first V-24 prototype was written off in a flight-test accident, apparently due to pilot error. The loss did not hinder flight-test efforts for the V-24, which proceeded at a pretty fast pace using the second prototype and a batch of ten pre-series helicopters for use in the development and evaluation programme. Five of these pre-series V-24s were built at Mil's own experimental plant at Panki (Aviation Plant No. 329) while the rest were produced by the Progress plant at Arsenyev in Russia's Far East (Aviation Plant No. 116);

The second V-24 prototype seen in flight. It features stub wings with no anhedral and lacks ATGM launchers. (Mil MHP)

the first example of this batch took to the air as early as 1971. One of the Arsenyev-built helicopters was intended for use as a flying laboratory for the new Shturm-V ATGMS system and another example was intended for static tests.

A huge number of teething troubles are reported to have surfaced during the test and evaluation phase of the V-24 prototype and pre-series batch machines; among these was "Dutch roll" – pronounced oscillations in yaw and roll axis occurring at speeds in excess of 108kt (200km/h) with the autopilot disengaged – as well as excessive in-flight vibrations and poor yaw stability.

In a bid to improve the latter the auxiliary wings, which initially lacked anhedral, were redesigned at 12 degrees anhedral.

The initial positioning of the ATGM launch rails on the fuselage was also considered unsuitable and to compromise flight safety due to the very high probability of collision between already-separated missiles and the helicopter; in consequence, the launch rails were relocated on to the stub-wings' endplates.

Another major design alteration was made after it became clear in initial tests that the available space was insufficient to accommodate the heavy, bulky Raduga-F ATGM guidance system as well as the machine gun turret; consequently, the forward fuselage was lengthened slightly, receiving a sharper profile. In addition, the end-user required that the WSO cockpit was also equipped with flight controls, which were to be used in the event that the pilot was disabled.

The then very new Klimov TV3-117 engine also initially proved to be a rather troublesome piece of kit – it tended to be prone to compressor surges, necessitating extensive reworking of the compressor stages. Another serious shortcoming of the new engine was its very low time between overhauls (TBO) – set out at only 50 hours due to reliability concerns.

Development of the V-24's armament systems also proved to be a major technical issue since the four-barrelled 12.7mm YakB-12.7 machine gun and its USPU-24 remotely-controlled turret saw notably protracted development and the system eventually turned out to be heavier and bulkier than expected. Hopeless delays were also experienced with the development and putting into service of the new 9M114 Shturm-V ATGM system, which therefore could not be used on the initial production helicopters.

The V-24, still in a partially complete weapon system configuration but already incorporating the full list of design alterations conceived after the initial flight-test stage, eventually entered its state testing and evaluation phase with the Soviet Air Force Research Test Institute in June 1970, which was completed within a year and a half. However, production of the new combat helicopter type followed the usual Soviet procurement practice as it was initiated in 1970, well before completion of the state testing and evaluation effort.

The A-10 was a record-breaking derivative of the Mi-24 used in the mid-1970s for setting various records approved by the Fédération Aéronautique Internationale, in Class E (helicopters). The most famous of these is the speed record of 199.13kt (368.4km/h) set by Gurgen Karapetyan, Mil's famous chief pilot, over an 8/13.5nm (15/25km) course near Moscow on 21 September 1978 (this was broken eight years later by a Westland Lynx with the BERP main rotor system). The aircraft used for the record-breaking flights was taken from the pre-production batch and the modifications made to the fuselage chiefly aimed at reducing weight as much as possible. There were several prototypes and experimental versions based on the Mi-24A – one of these was equipped with a fenestron-type tail rotor but tests showed the arrangement provided no benefit compared with the original design. The Mi-24M multi-role naval version offered in 1970 only ever existed on paper. The Mi-24BMT minesweeping derivative, lacking armour protection, armament and stub-wings and equipped with a trawling device and additional fuel tank, was built and tested in 1973 but was not approved for in-service use.

Introduction into service

The first production helicopters, designated Mi-24A (*Izdeliye* 245), entered service with the Voronezh-based branch of the Soviet Air Force's 4th Combat Training and Aircrew Conversion Centre in 1970. These machines were utilised to develop and further improve the combat deployment of the Mi-24 as well as for the conversion training of instructor pilots and aircrews for the front-line units to be re-equipped with the *Hind*. The first front-line Soviet Air Force unit to take the Mi-24A on strength was the 319th Red Banner Independent Helicopter Regiment in the Far Eastern Military District, based at Chernigovka, near the city of Vladivostok and not far from the Arsenyev production plant. Other Soviet Air Force front-line independent helicopter regiments to take the Mi-24A on strength were stationed at Brody and Raukhovka (Ukraine), Parchim and Stendal (East Germany), Pruzhani (Byelorussia) and Mogocha (Russia).

The independent helicopter regiments of the Army Aviation branch were composed of three or four squadrons, each with up to 20 helicopters. Two of

The Mil-24A-10 was a record-breaking derivative, with its most famous achievement being breaking the helicopter world speed record of 199.13kt (368.4km/h) set over an 8/13.5nm (15/25km) course near Moscow on 21 September 1978. (Mil MHP)

A Soviet Army propaganda photo dating from the 1970s, showing an Mi-24A over a moving tank column. The *Hind* was designed to support ground troops in offensive and defensive operations, to escort ground convoys and transport helicopters, and to destroy enemy tanks and other armoured vehicles. (Alexander Mladenov archive)

the squadrons were equipped with attack helicopters and the other one or two with transport types. In the early 1980s there were as many as 15 regiments constituting a fleet of no fewer than 400 Mi-24s. By 1989, the Mi-24 was in service with some 44 independent helicopter regiments of the Army Aviation (each of these provided with one or two *Hind*-equipped squadrons) and no less than 40 independent squadrons (each of these with between three and twelve Mi-24s of various variants, including the NBC reconnaissance and the fire correction ones).

In addition to Army Aviation, in the 1980s the *Hind* was introduced into service with the aviation assets of the Ministry of the Interior (Internal Troops Service) and the Federal Border Guard Service. After the breakup of the Soviet Union the Soviet Army Aviation attack helicopter fleet was distributed among the newly independent states. Russia, the juridical successor of the former Soviet Union inherited the largest fleet and today the Russian Air Force (Army Aviation Branch) has some ten independent helicopter regiments, each provided with one Mi-24 squadron (the fleet is a mixture of Mi-24V, Mi-24P and Mi-24PN machines) with an active inventory of around 200 units. The Mi-24 is also in service with the 344th Aircrew Conversion and Combat Training Centre of Army Aviation at Torzhok as well as with the Sizran Military Institute, for advanced pilot training.

VARIANTS

Mi-24A/B

The original Mi-24A (NATO *Hind-A*) became operational with the Soviet Air Force in 1972 though it was always regarded as nothing more than an interim variant and as such was never formally accepted into Soviet service. The Mi-24 is said to have demonstrated a disappointingly low combat effectiveness due to the inherent shortcomings of its main weapons system –

 This Russian Air Force (Army Aviation Branch) Mi-24V gunship wears the two-tone disruptive scheme standard for Soviet and Russian Army Aviation in the 1980s and 1990s. It also carries an excellence-award insignia on the nose, applied in the same orange colour as the tactical code. This Mi-24V belongs to the 485th Independent Helicopter Regiment (*Otdelny Vertoletny Polk*). Based until mid-1991 at Merseburg in East Germany, the regiment then moved to nearby Brandis and by 1992 was eventually relocated to Alakurtti in Russia, subordinated to the Leningrad Military District. By the time it left Merseburg the regiment had 24 Mi-24Vs, six Mi-24Rs and six Mi-24Ks. The unit was disbanded in 1998 and its helicopters were transferred to other Russian Army Aviation helicopter regiments. The Mi-24V was the most popular version of the *Hind* in Soviet and Russian Army Aviation service and is still in widespread use in mixed attack squadrons of independent helicopter regiments together with the Mi-24P. This aircraft is armed with two B8V20 rocket pods each housing 20 S-8 rockets. The basic S-8 has a shaped-charge/fragmentation warhead while the improved S-8M and S-8KOM introduced warheads with enhanced fragmentation effects. The latter also has much improved armour penetration capabilities at ranges up to 1,310ft (400m), while its fragments remain lethal within a radius of 39ft (12m).

The Mi-24B was a vastly improved Mi-24A derivative which retained the Mi-24A's front fuselage but introduced the USPU-24 turret with the YakB-12.7 four-barrelled machine gun, together with the much-improved 9M17P Falanga-PV ATGM system. (Mil MHP)

the 9M17M Falanga-M ATGM. This missile system required a skilled operator to achieve a hit, and its probability of kill (PoK) was only 30 per cent due to the relatively ineffective manual guidance method.

Pilots also raised a plethora of rather serious complaints, mainly concerning the poor visibility allowed by the Mi-24A's conventional enclosed wide flight-deck, especially on the right-hand side, while the cockpit armour protection was also considered to be very poor. Initially, TV3-117 Series 1 engines were used to power the Mi-24A but as noted, these had a very short TBO. The improved Series 2 engines, with an increased TBO of 300 hours, were made available for installation on the Mi-24A not before 1973. The *Hind-A* also suffered from a relatively ineffective tail rotor on the starboard side, inherited from the Mi-8T/P; this design proved unable to provide consistent enough control authority in strong crosswind conditions. In an effort to eliminate this shortcoming, in 1974 the tail rotor was redesigned and moved to port and its direction of rotation reversed – switching from pusher to tractor configuration. Initial operating experience also prompted strengthening of the tail boom by inserting new reinforcement ribs.

The Mi-24U was the conversion training derivative of the Mi-24A with the WSO cockpit redesigned for use by an instructor pilot, equipped with a full set of controls and instruments. The ATGM targeting system and the machine gun were deleted, although the capability of using rocket pods was retained. This version entered production in 1973 and together with the Mi-24A continued in manufacture at the Arsenyev plant until 1974.

A total of 240 Mi-24A/Us rolled out of the assembly hall and a small proportion of them even exported to a few friendly Third World states such as Afghanistan, Vietnam and Ethiopia.

The Mi-24U was the conversion training derivative of the Mi-24A, stripped of ATGM capability and lacking the nose 12.7mm machine gun. (Mil MHP)

The Mi-24B (*Izdeliye* 241), the second combat version, retained the Mi-24A's wide flight deck but introduced the USPU-24 turret with the YakB-12.7 four-barrelled machine gun, together with the much improved 9M17P Falanga-PV ATGM system with semi-automatic command line-of-sight (SACLOS) guidance for a better PoK (quoted as up to 80 per cent) and reduced workload on the WSO. However, this version was also considered an interim one and as such it saw a very limited production run, being rapidly replaced on the Arsenyev assembly line by a more modern *Hind* derivative with an all-new gunship-style forward fuselage.

Mi-24D

The Mi-24D, also known as *Izdeliye* 246 (NATO *Hind-D*), was another interim version which introduced the definitive stepped tandem cockpits forward of the engine inlets, with the pilot at the rear and the WSO in front. This new layout was much appreciated by pilots as it provided an unobstructed field of view and considerably better protection. In addition, each cockpit was provided with a bullet-proof windscreen and rounded canopy. The pilot's cockpit featured a rearward-opening hinged door to starboard while the WSO's cockpit introduced a hinged canopy, opening to starboard. The Mi-24D – first design work on which started as early as in 1971 – also featured a semi-recessed nose landing-gear unit which was lengthened, giving the helicopter a pronounced nose-up attitude when on the ground.

A boom protruding in front of the WSO's cockpit with angle-of-attack and sideslip-angle vanes was installed for providing information necessary for precise weapon-aiming purposes. The fuel system was also modified to allow 500-litre fuel tanks to be carried under the stub wings. Initially, Mi-24Ds were produced without engine dust filters but such devices were added in 1975 in an effort to reduce tear and wear on the TV3-117 engines due to ingested dust and sand during operations from unprepared landing sites. In 1977, the TV3-117 Series 3 engines, boasting an extended to 750 hours TBO, were introduced on the Mi-24D.

The Mi-24D introduced a significantly redesigned airframe, but was still regarded as an interim version retaining the Mi-24B's weapons system. The first two Mi-24Ds were converted from early-production Mi-24As in 1972 and also retained the starboard tail rotor. The new *Hind* version underwent its state testing phase between February and November 1974 but had already entered production at the Arsenyev plant in 1973, not long after production of this derivative at Aviation Plant No. 168 at Rostov-on-Don; the latter was tasked with manufacturing *Hind-Ds* for export customers. Warsaw Pact member states received helicopters almost identical to those built for

The Mi-24D was the first *Hind* version to introduce the definitive stepped tandem cockpits forward of the engine inlets, with the pilot to the rear and the WSO in front. (Alexander Mladenov)

A Slovak Air Force Mi-24D, seen in a strafing pass using the 12.7mm YakB-12.7 machine gun which has a rate of fire of 4,000rpm and a muzzle velocity of 2,650ft/s (810m/s). (Miroslav Gyürösi, via Alexander Mladenov)

Soviet Army Aviation, while Third World client states were supplied with an Mi-24D derivative designated the Mi-25, with a lower standard of equipment and avionics.

The Mi-24D was formally accepted into service with the Soviet Air Force on 29 March 1976 and remained in production at the Arsenyev plant until 1977, while in Rostov-on-Don this variant continued in production for export customers until the mid-1980s. As many as 350 examples were produced at the former location and no fewer than 300 additional Mi-24D/-25s rolled off the production line at the latter one.

The Mi-24DU (*Izdeliye* 249) was the conversion training derivative of the Mi-24D designed in line with the concept proven during development of the Mi-24U. The Mi-24DU, just like its predecessor the Mi-24U, had the Mi-24D's WSO cockpit converted for use by an instructor pilot. The Mi-24DU had the ATGM system and the gun turret deleted but retaining the capability of firing rockets and dropping bombs.

A close-up of the Mi-24D's USPU-24 under-nose turret with 12.7mm YakB-12.7 machine gun. (Alexander Mladenov)

A 9M17P Falanga-V missile on the launch rails of a Hungarian Air Force Mi-24D. (Miroslav Gyürösi, via Alexander Mladenov)

Mi-24V and Mi-24P

The Mi-24V, also known as *Izdeliye* 242 (NATO *Hind-E*) is the most popular version of the *Hind*, also exported worldwide under the Mi-35 designation; it is still in low-rate production at the plant in Rostov-on-Don, now named Rostvertol. The *Hind-E's* fuselage is externally similar to that of the Mi-24D, but this version at last introduced the new 9M114 Shturm-V (NATO AT-6 *Spiral*) ATGM system and improved equipment and avionics. Another major improvement was the integration of the TV3-117V engine in the early 1980s. This new TV3-117 derivative, rated at 2,225shp (1,660kW), was purposely designed for hot-and-high operations, retaining its maximum power rating of 2,200shp up to 7,216ft (2,200m) and up to 30 degrees C at sea level. In the early 1980s the TV3-117V was also installed on late-production Mi-24Ds destined for export customers.

The Mi-24V could use a considerably wider array of unguided weapons than the Mi-24D and introduced the more modern ASP-17V automatic gunsight for the pilot. Externally, the *Hind-E* can be distinguished from the Hind-D by its modified wingtip launchers and the enlarged undernose antenna pod on the port side, with a more rounded front end, which is used for the Shturm-V ATGM guidance. In addition, a second non-retractable landing light is installed on the port side of the nose. Late-production Mi-24Vs were equipped with the SPO-15 radar warning receiver system, with its large forward-facing antennae installed in characteristic 'horns' aft of the rear cockpit or between the two cockpits; the latter arrangement is observed on the export *Hind-Es* only.

In the early 1980s, all existing Mi-24Vs and Mi-24Ds received the ASO-2V chaff/flare-dispenser units, used for protection against heat-seeking missiles; initially six 32-round units were installed under the tail boom while the late production machines introduced ASO-2Vs in packs on the aft fuselage sides. The L-116V-11E Lipa Infrared (IR) 'disco-light' jammer was another example of newly-added equipment to protect the helicopter against heat-seeking missiles, installed aft of the main rotor hub. The third component of the suite of defensive aids against heat-seeking missiles comprised EVU IR

The Mi-24V is still the most popular version of the *Hind*, exported worldwide under the Mi-35 designation. Its fuselage is externally similar to that of the Mi-24D but the derivative used the new 9M114 Shturm-V (NATO AT-6 *Spiral*) ATGM system along with improved equipment and avionics. (Alexander Mladenov)

radiation-suppression devices for the engines, which mix the exhaust gases with cold air and were introduced in 1984.

In 1986 the Mi-24V was tested with multiple ATGM launchers, allowing the helicopter to carry as many as 16 Shturm-V missiles. In 1985, an Mi-24V was tested with a rearward-firing NSVT-12.7 Utyos machine gun and additional armour protection for the pilot and WSO. Tests showed that this modification was unsuitable due to the shift in the centre of gravity and to exhaust-gas contamination of the rear-gunner's position. The Mi-24V's weapons suite was expanded in the mid-1980s with the introduction of GUV weapons pods containing either one 12.7mm and two 7.62mm rapid-fire machine guns or one AGS-17 30mm grenade-launcher and two 7.62mm rapid-fire machine guns. UPK-23-250 gun pods housing the highly accurate

The Mi-24V's tube-launched 9M114 Shturm-V missiles are carried on the wing endplates. This 1970s-vintage missile has a real-world launch range of 0.8–1.88nm (1.5–3.5km). Combat experience showed that firing precisely at the maximum range of 2.7nm (5km) would be difficult for the Shturm-V due to problems associated with detection and positive identification of the target. (Alexander Mladenov)

and lethal GSh-23L 23mm rapid-fire guns were also introduced, along with powerful S-8 rockets fired from 20-round pods. The Mi-24V could also carry 240mm S-24 and 122mm S-13 rockets and KMG-U bomblet/mine dispensers. In the latter half of the 1980s the Mi-24 received the capability to use the R-60 (AA-8 *Aphid*) air-to-air missile. The R-60 was not used widely on the Mi-24 but a few helicopters within regiments stationed close to borders were upgraded to use the missile with a view to use in low-latitude air defence against slow-flying targets which could not be effectively intercepted by jet fighters. Iraqi and Polish *Hinds* reportedly also gained the capability to use the R-60.

The Mi-24V prototype was constructed in 1973 using an early-production Mi-24D airframe, and the new version was formally introduced into the Soviet Air Force inventory together with the Mi-24D in March 1976. No fewer than 1,000 Mi-24Vs were produced at Arsenyev between 1976 and 1986 for the Soviet Armed Forces, Ministry of Interior and the Border Guard Service, while another 400-plus examples rolled off the line at Rostov-on-Don, destined for export customers.

A view inside the pilot's cockpit (the rear position) on the Mi-24V shows that it is dominated by a large navigation display and the ASP-17V automatic sight. Above the sight is the display panel for the SPO-15 radar homing warning receiver. (Alexander Mladenov)

The Mi-24P, also known as *Izdeliye* 243 (NATO *Hind-F*), has a fuselage and systems similar to those of the Mi-24V but introduced the powerful 30mm, 470-round GSh-2-30 cannon replacing the flexible YaKB-12.7 machine gun. The large-calibre twin-barrelled forward-firing fixed gun is installed within a semi-cylindrical pack on the starboard side of the front fuselage. The barrel section is provided with extended flashguards to protect the helicopter's front fuselage from the flames and blast generated by the very powerful cannon. The underside of the *Hind-F's* nose is smoothly faired above and forward of the sensors.

As many as 620 Mi-24Ps were built at the Arsenyev plant between 1981 and 1989, although newly-built gun-armed *Hind-Fs* are still offered to export customers by Rostvertol under the Mi-35P designation.

A view of the WSO's cockpit (the forward position) on the Mi-24V. It is fitted with sighting and guidance equipment for the 9M114 Shturm-V ATGM and the USPU-24 machine gun turret. (Alexander Mladenov)

B MI-24P

The Mi-24 has a fuselage of all-metal pod-and-boom construction, with 5mm integral steel armour on the forward fuselage. Pilot and weapons operator are provided with armoured seats and individual canopies. Each cockpit has an optically flat armoured windshield with wiper. The powerplant consists of two Klimov TV3-117V turboshafts, a 'high-altitude' version of the tried-and-tested TV3-117 series, maintaining a power rating of 2,200shp (1,617kW) up to 9,840ft (3,000m). Engines are installed side-by-side above the cabin, with output shafts driving the main rotor shaft rearward through a combining gearbox. The Mi-24P's GSh-30K cannon is a precise and lethal weapon firing projectiles with a muzzle velocity of 2,952ft/s (900m/s); they retain flat trajectory at a range of up to 3,283ft (1,000m). The gun is said to be particularly effective when used from an altitude exceeding 656ft (200m) in horizontal flight or a shallow dive, and it is usually employed in combined attack passes, with rockets launched first and then onboard artillery used to inflict further damage on the target.

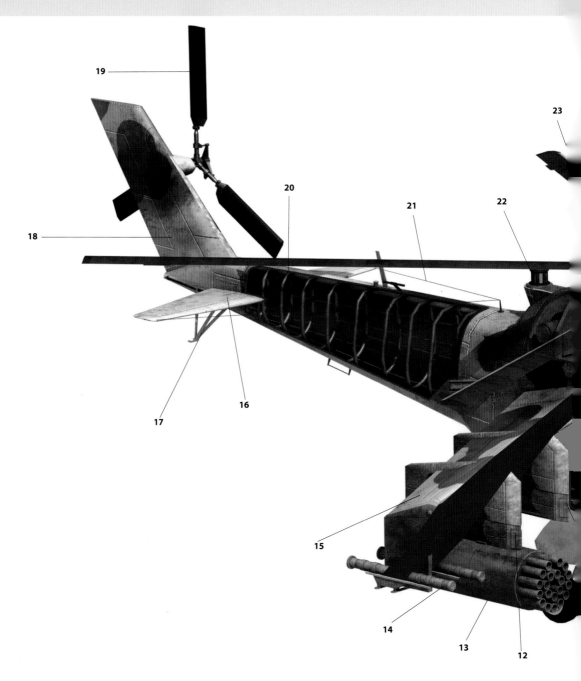

Key

1. Armoured glass windscreen of the pilot's cockpit
2. Armoured glass windscreen of the WSO's cockpit
3. Air data sensor boom
4. Antenna pod for radio-command line used for the guidance of the Shturm-V anti-tank guided missile
5. A pod housing the Raduga-F optical guidance system used for tracking the flightpath of the Shturm-V anti-tank guided missile
6. 30mm GSh-2-30 (GSh-30K) twin-barrel cannon with 470 rounds
7. Nose landing gear leg
8. Lower door segment in open position
9. Main cabin seating for eight fully armed troops
10. Starboard wing inner pylon
11. Starboard main landing gear leg
12. Starboard wing inner pylon
13. B-8V20 20-round rocket pack for launching the S-8 80mm rockets
14. 9M114 Shturm-V (AT-6 *Spiral*) anti-tank missile launch tube
15. Stub wing
16. Starboard all moving tailplane
17. Tail bumper
18. Tail fin
19. Tail rotor
20. Tail boom frame construction
21. HF radio aerial cable
22. L-116V-11E Lipa infra-red suppressor
23. Main rotor blade
24. Main reduction gearbox
25. Starboard engine exhaust duct
26. Main rotor hub
27. Oil cooler
28. Forward facing antenna fairing for the SPO-15 radar warning receiver
29. Starboard TV3-117V turboshaft engine
30. Starboard engine air intake duct/debris extractor
31. Pilot's armoured seat
32. WSO's armoured seat

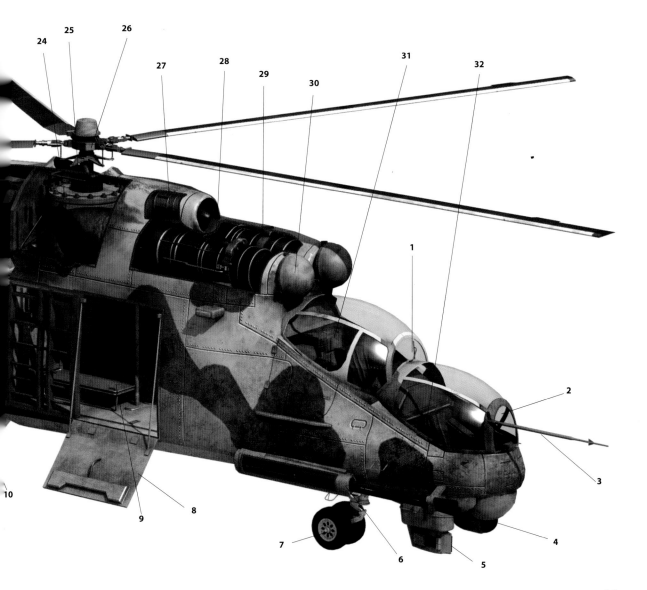

The Mi-24P is the ultimate *Hind* gunship derivative armed with the powerful 30mm GSh-30K cannon. This has two firing modes – rapid or slow, with 2,460rpm or 300rpm respectively – and is provided with 250 rounds of ammunition. (Mikhail Lavrov, via Alexander Mladenov)

The Mi-24VP, also known as *Izdeliye* 258, is another Mi-24V derivative armed with a 23mm cannon instead of the YaKB-12.7 flexible machine gun. This derivative introduced the twin-barrelled GSh-23 cannon mounted in the NPPU-24 turret in the nose. A prototype was first flown in 1985 but testing proved a protracted undertaking due to problems associated with the gun integration. As a result, the Mi-24VP started production not before 1989 and only 25 examples rolled off the line at Arsenyev.

Specialised NBC and artillery fire-correction *Hinds*

Two special-mission derivatives of the *Hind* were produced in relatively large numbers in the 1980s. The first of them is the Mi-24R (*Izdeliye* 2462), known within NATO as *Hind-G1*, used for nuclear, biological and chemical (NBC) warfare purposes. It carries equipment for measuring radiation and chemical/biological contamination, transmitting the information to the ground via a datalink. Air samples are taken through a ventral intake protruding from the forward fuselage. The cockpits and cabin have much-improved NBC protection and soil samples can be collected using remote-controlled mechanical grabbers installed on the stub-wing endplates. Consoles are provided for two NBC-equipment operators in the cabin. The *Hind-G1* is stripped of guided weapons capability, but retains the nose machine gun turret and rockets under the stub wings.

An Mi-24R prototype was constructed in 1978 by converting one early production Mi-24V, and as many as 152 examples were produced at the Arsenyev plant between 1983 and 1989. In 1995, an upgraded version designated as the Mi-24RA was tested for the first time.

The Mi-24K (*Izdeliye* 201) *Hind-G2* is the artillery fire-correction derivative of the *Hind*. Like the Mi-24R, it also lacks guided weapons capability but is endowed with a powerful camera suite for spotting targets on the battlefield, operated by the WSO. This comprises the computer-controlled Ruta system with an undernose Iris EO sight and radio datalink,

The GSh-30K twin-barrelled, forward-firing, fixed 30mm cannon, aimed through the ASP-17 reflector sight, is said to be a highly lethal and fairly precise weapon, firing highly destructive 390-gram projectiles of fragmentation/high-explosive/incendiary/tracer type. (Rostvertol)

while within the cabin a large AFA-100 oblique photo camera is installed. The Mi-24K lacks the port cabin door, instead, the port side sports a large camera window with optically flat glass. The Mi-24K prototype was converted from an Mi-24V airframe; it was completed in 1979 and 163 production examples were built between 1983 and 1989.

Another highly specialised version was produced, dubbed the Mi-24TECh, which was a flying laboratory for checking the Mi-24's onboard equipment and carrying out scheduled inspections in field conditions. It was developed in 1981 at the plant at Rostov-on-Don.

The Mi-24K is a specialised *Hind* derivative based on the Mi-24V, designed for artillery fire-correction purposes. No examples of this version were exported during Soviet times, and only two helicopters of this version were exported in 2001 by Ukraine to the former Yugoslav republic of Macedonia. (Alexander Mladenov)

UPGRADES

Mi-24PN

The Russian Air Force (RuAF) has so far elected to field an austere upgrade for the cannon-armed Mi-24P. The procurement order is presumed to have covered no more than 18 aircraft. This interim-upgraded *Hind* version, designated the Mi-24PN ("N" standing for *Nochnoy* or "night-capable") was fielded in an effort to meet an urgent night-operating capability for homeland defence missions.

The Mi-24PN introduced NVG-compatible cockpits and a BREO-24 avionics suite integrating one LCD colour display in each cockpit as well as a precise navigation system with satellite navigation receiver. It also introduced a number of powerplant, airframe and rotor refinements. The first batch of five Mi-24PNs overhauled and life-extended by Rostvertol was handed over to the RuAF in January 2004 and about eight additional machines were delivered in 2005 and 2006.

The Mil Moscow Helicopter Plant (Mil MHP), as the design bureau is now known, stressed the claim that the overall combat capabilities of the Mi-24PN increased 1.5–1.7 times compared with that of the "vanilla" Mi-24P. This becomes possible thanks to the introduction of the new night-capable fire-control system built around the rather basic 9S47N Zarevo III gyrostabilised night-vision (NV) sighting system, made by the Russian company Krasnodar Optical-Mechanical Plant as a follow-on development of the Nokturn NV device used in main battle tanks. The Zarevo system was initially intended to be housed in a pod carried under the wing but in the event the system was installed in a protruding "chin" mount. It integrates

In January 2004 the Russian Air Force took on strength its first five production-upgraded Mi-24PNs with enhanced night-operating capabilities. (Rostvertol, via Alexander Mladenov)

an IR sensor coupled with laser rangefinder and IR goniometer (a device used for ATGM guidance), integrated with the standard Raduga-Sh radio-guidance system.

Low-level flying at night became possible thanks to the cockpit lighting adaptation for use with the Russian-made OVN-1 or GEO ONV-1 night-vision goggles (NVGs), which allow flight at night down to 164ft (50m).

The first Mi-24PNs entered service with the RuAF 334th Aircrew Conversion and Combat Training Centre at Torzhok, tasked with training instructors and front-line pilots in NV combat operations, in early 2004; in the same year a four-aircraft flight was taken on strength by the 487th Independent Helicopter Regiment stationed near the city of Budyonnovsk in southern Russia, not far from the troubled autonomous republic of Chechnya.

In February 2004 it was widely announced in the Russian media that a foreign customer, later disclosed as Uganda, was interested in acquiring up to six Mi-24PNs. In the event only one Mi-24PN is understood to have been delivered to this African country.

KNEI-24/OPS-24-equipped upgraded *Hinds*

The comprehensive upgrade proposals by Mil MHP for both the Mi-24V and Mi-24P comprised "building blocks" or upgrade modules – numbered Blocks 1 to 5 – that can be implemented either independently from one other or together, depending on customer's operational requirements and budgets.

A comprehensive service life-cycle extension programme based on thorough inspections of the actual condition of each individual airframe is included in the Block 1 module, while Block 2 deals with the rotor system replacement. The main rotor hub and composite blades of the Mi-28N, as well as an X-shaped tail rotor, are installed. For this block there is also an option to introduce the uprated Klimov VK-2500 turboshaft, which would result in noticeable performance gains in 'hot-and-high' operating conditions.

Block 3 encompasses a good many airframe refinements such as shortened stub-wings and nonretractable landing gear. The latter, for instance, is said to cause a reduction of only 6kt (11km/h) in maximum level speed. The total weight reduction thanks to all these airframe refinements is some 1,300lb (600kg) which, together with Block 2 improvements, results in an increase in maximum service ceiling by 985ft (300m) – to 10,170ft (3,100m) in standard conditions – while the rate of climb increases to 2,480ft/min (12.4m/s).

Block 4 calls for a host of weapons suite enhancements, the main one being the introduction of the 9M120 Ataka-V system, with up to eight missiles on two wingtip launchers; this was purposely developed for the Mi-28 in the 1980s. The supersonic Ataka missile boasts a maximum range of 3.2nm (5.8km) and its tandem warhead boasts an armour penetration capability of up to 33in (850mm). For self-defence and operations against unmanned aerial vehicles and other helicopters, the 9M39 Igla-V missile is offered in twin launcher packs. It is also possible in this block to replace the Mi-24V's 12.7-mm YakB-12.7 four-barrelled gun with a 23mm GSh-23 twin-barrelled cannon mounted in the NPPU-23 turret, as originally designed for the Mi-24VP derivative in the late 1980s. The upgraded *Hind* is also capable of using the large and relatively long-range S-13 122mm rockets, carried in five-round pods.

Block 5, the final and most expensive set of improvements originally offered by Mil MHP, introduces day/night and adverse weather operating capability.

A much better-equipped upgraded derivative of the 30mm gun-armed *Hind-F* – the Mi-24PK-2, incorporating some of the Block 1 to 5 features – failed to enter service with the RuAF but is still on offer for export customers. It, together with its machine gun-armed cousin the Mi-24VK-2, introduced the KNEI-24 affordable digital avionics package developed by the Russkaya Avionika company and the OPS-24N day/night targeting system developed by Mil. The core feature of the latter is the UOMZ GOES-342 optronic payload, integrating a forward-looking infrared (FLIR), TV camera, laser rangefinder and IR goniometer (a device allowing night-time Shturm-V and Ataka-V ATGM employment); low-level TV camera is optional. The GOES-342 FLIR device facilitates detection of tank-size targets at night at distances of 2.2–3.2nm (4–6km) and during the day the TV facility has a range of up to 5.4nm (10km) – considered adequate for employment of the Ataka-V ATGM system.

The cockpits of the Mi-24PK-2 and VK-2, as well as the Mi-35M, are compatible with the Geofizika-NV GEO-ONV-1-01 Gen III night-vision goggles, which have a Field of View of 40 degrees and target-detection range of up to 3,300ft (1,000m).

Mi-35M

In July 2006, the *Servicio Aéreo del Ejército Venezolano* (Venezuelan Army Aviation Service) became the latest *Hind* operator. It was in fact the launch customer for the ultimate 21st-century *Hind* – the most modern derivative of the Mi-24 in production, designated the Mi-35M. This is a newly-built day/night-capable attack helicopter boasting KNEI-24 and OPS-24 avionics as well as a host of significant airframe/powerplant/rotor-system improvements as covered in the Block 1 to 5 upgrade modules.

The Mi-24PN's new fire-control system is built around the bulky Zarevo gyrostabilised sighting system, derived from a tank nightsight, which is housed in a distinctive protruding chin mount. (Rostvertol, via Alexander Mladenov)

The Mi-35M represents the end result of an effort over several years by Mil MHP. It was promoted for the first time in 1995 as a high-end upgrade package for both the old *Hind* versions and newly-built increased-performance machines, but customers were initially reluctant to come forward en masse. Eventually it was Venezuela, a payable and motivated foreign state, that became the launch customer for this newly-built derivative: it ordered ten Mi-35Ms, which were delivered in 2006 and 2007 and received the local designation Caribe.

In late 2009 the Brazilian Air Force took on strength the first examples of a batch of 12 newly-built Mi-35Ms, ordered in 2008. The Brazilian contract exceeds US$160m; these Mi-35Ms are in a configuration said to be generally

The Mi-24PK-2 is an Mi-24P upgraded with the KNEI-24 and OPS-24 mission systems for day/night operations. However, the Russian Air Force is still reluctant to accept this upgrade into service due to the lack of funding. (Mil MHP)

similar to that of the Venezuelan *Hinds*, although incorporating some Western and Israeli avionics components.

Israeli upgrade proposals

Israel Aerospace Industries (IAI), with its Mission 24 upgrade package, succeeded in securing the first-ever major upgrade contract for the *Hind*. IAI's package, widely advertised since 1999 as an affordable integration of observation/sighting, navigation, self-defence and self-protection equipment proven in real-world operational conditions, was selected by the Indian Air Force, which is the only known customer for Mission 24 so far. The Indian deal comprised 25 upgrade kits under a US$20m contract signed in 1998.

IAI's Mission 24 upgrade package is built around a Mil Std 1553B digital databus, and the heart of the upgrade is a single mission computer developed with IAI's MLM systems integration division alongside the multi-mission digital optronic gyrostabilised payload, the HMOSP. Both Mission 24 cockpits are NVG-compatible, and the crew has the option to use IAI's advanced NVG set with built-in monocular display, on which navigation and targeting information can be presented.

Navigational improvements introduced with the Mission 24 include a global positioning system (GPS) receiver integrated with the existing DISS-15D Doppler sensor, and a 3-D digital map display is also on offer. Both the HMOSP and YakB-12.7 gun are slaved to the pilot's line of sight through the use of a helmet-mounted sensor, and the machine gun can be slaved to the HMOSP as well. A self-defence capability is also on offer, comprising Israeli-made chaff/flare-dispenser units and Elta radar/laser/missile-warning systems. The total weight of the new systems is about 111lb (50kg).

Elbit Systems is another Israeli company known for

The day/night-capable Mi-35M, for which the Venezuelan Army Aviation Service was the launch customer. This derivative is armed with the Ataka-V ATGM and features nonretractable landing gear. (Tina Shaposhnikova/Rostvertol)

being very active in the field of *Hind* upgrades worldwide. It has won a few upgrade projects; the first of these is the introduction of night-operating ATGM capability and a comprehensive self-defence suite (based on missile approach warning receivers) for Sri Lankan Air Force Mi-24Vs and Mi-24Ps – five each in 2004 and 2005. The Sri Lankan Mi-24s also introduced the CoMPASS IV (Compact Multi-Purpose Advanced Stabilised System IV) electro-optical system for day and night reconnaissance, surveillance and targeting.

A view into the weapons operator's cockpit (the forward position) of the upgrade of the Mi-35M, with a display added to assist day and night targeting, with the new ATGM control console beneath it. (Alexander Mladenov)

The second known customer of Elbit Systems is the air force of the Former Yugoslav Republic of Macedonia (FYROM), for four Mi-24Vs upgraded to various standards under the so-called Alexander project. The first stage of the FYROM programme encompassed the integration of the ANVIS/HUD-24 system (a helmet-mounted display and sighting system combined with the AN/AVS-7 NVG system), and the introduction of cockpit NVG compatibility as well as a Trimble GPS receiver. The second stage introduced navigation, communication and IFF equipment to NATO and International Civil Aviation Organization standards, new self-defence aids, and two multifunctional displays for the moving digital map and for information derived from the CoMPASS IV multi-sensor turret and HOCAS controls. The third upgrade stage called for the introduction of a head-mounted cueing system for both the sensor turret and the YakB-12.7 machine gun. A similar, if not the same, upgrade standard was also adopted by the Georgian Air Force in the mid-2000s for six of its *Hind-Es*.

A view of the pilot's cockpit of the Mi-35M, upgraded with a pair of LCD displays. (Alexander Mladenov)

ATE's *Super Hind* line

The South African company Advanced Technologies and Engineering (ATE) is another non-Russian firm that has carried out a successful *Hind* upgrade programme. An export order covering up to 40 Mi-24s was signed in 1999, and the first upgraded helicopters – dubbed *Super Hinds* – were supplied to the customer nation, Algeria, in the same year. An additional order from Algeria announced by ATE in late 2002 calls for the further upgrade to an enhanced standard of an undisclosed number of helicopters.

The *Super Hind* core package is currently being offered in two main versions. The first of these, dubbed Mk II, aims to enhance the capability of the Mi-35P 30mm cannon-armed helicopters and retains the original

The Mi-35M is armed with a twin-barrelled 23mm GSh-23 cannon, as tried and tested already on the Mi-24VP, and is capable of operating at night thanks to the integration of the high-tech UOMZ GOES-342 optronic targeting/surveillance payload with IR, TV and LLTV (optional) channels. (Alexander Mladenov)

Russian-built weapons, introducing a new observation/targeting and precise-navigation package. The second upgrade version, the Mk III, boasts an all-new weapons-control system, with the 12.7mm four-barrelled YakB-12.7 machine gun replaced by a 20mm cannon and the Falanga-P/Shturm-V ATGMs with the Kentron ZT35 *Ingwe* ("Leopard") laserbeam-riding missile.

The core avionics system, which is at the heart of all three of ATE's upgrade standards, is based on that developed for the South African Denel AH-2 *Rooivalk* ("Kestrel") attack helicopter. The system comprises an ATE-produced mission computer interfaced with various onboard systems and is responsible for all navigation/weapons-delivery data processing. The upgrade also adds NVG-compatible cockpit and formation lights plus a steerable infrared landing light and a Kentron Cumulus Argos 550 gyrostabilised multisensor payload with autotracker, TV camera, FLIR and laser rangefinder.

Other components of the core Mk II/Mk III system are the new head-up display, new NVG-friendly navigation displays in both cockpits, and a new self-defence system with programmable Vinten chaff/flare-dispenser units.

The more sophisticated Mk III package combines the core system with a host of additional high-tech features, such as the Archer R2 HMS system developed by Kentron, which allows for either crew-member to cue the Argus 550 multisensor payload and a high-rate-of-slew turret with the F2 20mm 840-round gun, housed in cheek fairings.

One of the most important elements in the *Super Hind* Mk III's operational-capability enhancement package is the new Ingwe ATGM: eight such missiles can be carried on two four-round launchers on the modified wingtips. In addition, the helicopter can carry a wide range of Russian- and South African-made rocket pods and free-fall bombs.

The new agile derivative now known as the *Super Hind* Mk V, and formerly the *Agile Hind*, was unveiled in mock-up form at the Africa Aerospace and Defence exhibition at Cape Town, South Africa, in September 2006. This introduced an all-new front fuselage that abandons the distinctive 'double-bubble' stepped cockpit layout: now, the pilot sits in front and

C 1. A Cuban Air Force Mi-24D. A batch of around 20 helicopters was delivered in 1984, followed by an unspecified number of Mi-24Vs. Little is known about the current state of the Cuban *Hind* fleet. There is evidence that some Cuban Mi-24s were outfitted with the LPG-150 winch installed above the port cabin door, presumably for use in search-and-rescue operations.

2. The Cyprus National Guard is among the latest *Hind* operators in Europe, in 2001–3 acquiring up to 12 newly-built Mi-35Ps with cockpits compatible with night-vision goggles and the capability to use the new 9M120 Ataka-V ATGM carried in eight-round launcher units. These *Hind-Fs* wear an overall gunmetal-grey colour scheme deemed especially suitable for night operations.

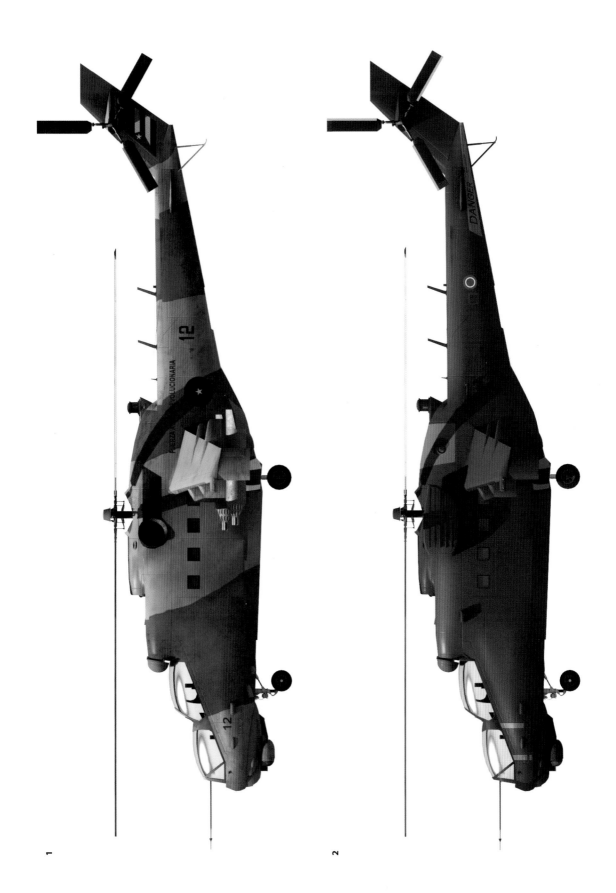

1

2

In 2004 the FYROM Air Force ordered an upgrade of four of its Mi-24Vs, to various standards under the so-called Alexander project. The first stage of the programme, completed in 2005, encompassed integration of the ANVIS/HUD-24 system – a helmet-mounted display and sighting system combined with the AN/AVS-7 night-vision goggles (NVG) system – and introduction of cockpit NVG compatibility as well as a Trimble GPS receiver. (Alexander Mladenov)

is provided with better visibility, while the WSO occupies the rear cockpit. This effort has saved weight in excess of 4,000lb (1,816kg), as new armour protection is centred on the crew members rather than the airframe.

SAGEM's *Hind* upgrade

Another company offering a viable Mi-24 avionics upgrade is France's SAGEM – a major avionics and systems manufacturer and integrator. At the 2001 Paris Air Show, the company proudly displayed an Mi-24P in Uzbek Air Force markings that boasted a variety of newly-added digital systems. It was reported that each cockpit was fitted with a single 6x6in colour display plus NVG-compatible lighting for use with SAGEM's own CN2H night-vision goggles, while the highly precise Sigma 95L navigation system combines inertial and GPS sensor inputs with the Mercator mapping module. A turret beneath the nose houses the modern Stryx payload, developed for the French Army's Eurocopter Tiger HAP combat and fire-support helicopter, which has FLIR, CCD TV and laser rangefinder-designator. It was widely reported at the show that SAGEM had won a contract to upgrade 12 Uzbek Air Force Mi-24s, in cooperation with local aircraft manufacturer TAPOiCh of Tashkent.

In 2008, SAGEM at last managed to enter the Ukrainian Mi-24 upgrade market when the French company was selected by the Ukrainian Ministry of Defence as the main supplier of avionics and integration services for a programme run by the local Aviacon helicopter maintenance company. SAGEM will supply avionics and NV equipment for the upgrade, while local companies such as Motor Sich and Promin will supply new engines and the Barrier ATGM system. An upgrade of the helicopter's self-defence suite will also be undertaken via installation of the new Andron Adros KT-01AV IR omnidirectional jammer, reported as being an effective system for disrupting the guidance of the latest generation of heat-seeking missiles.

HINDS IN ACTION

The Soviet campaign in Afghanistan, 1979–89

The Soviet Union's 'Afghan war campaign', as the conflict is known in today's Russia, proved a rather unforgiving trial for Army Aviation units engaged in supporting ground forces. It is of note that in the 1980s, 'Army Aviation' was used to denote a helicopter force used to perform missions at army level, the majority of these being assault transport and fire support, but actually operated by the Soviet Air Force.

ATE's *Sova-Attack* technology demonstrator was a *Super Hind* Mk III derivative aimed at East European Mi-24 operators. (Alexander Mladenov)

Soviet Army Aviation in Afghanistan took part in 416 large-scale offensive operations in support of land forces. In this situation, the old truth that the helicopter is the single most important weapon in counter-insurgency combat was demonstrated once again.

At the beginning only 110 helicopters were deployed in the war theatre, tasked with providing air support to the Soviet military contingent. They were grouped within the 40th Army, which managed to occupy Afghanistan in under two weeks. Ninety of the helicopters were transport-tasked Mi-8Ts; only six Mi-24A attack helicopters were deployed at the start of the campaign. However, two months after the beginning of the invasion the *Hind* fleet was strengthened by an additional 40 Mi-24Ds, provided in an effort to launch regular counter-insurgency operations across the country.

Flights, detachments and squadrons equipped with the Mi-24 were used to provide close air support (CAS) and escorts for transport helicopters during routine missions and for assault landing operations, as well as escort

A close-up of the *Super Hind's* Kentron Cumulus Argos 550 gyrostabilised multisensor payload with auto-tracker, TV camera, FLIR and laser rangefinder and the F2 20mm gun. (Alexander Mladenov)

The Mi-24 saw a great deal of operational use during the Soviet military involvement in Afghanistan between 1979 and 1989 and at least 122 examples were reported as lost in combat during the campaign. (Alexander Mladenov archive)

and protection from the air of ground-vehicle convoys supplying Soviet garrisons scattered throughout Afghanistan. The Mi-24s were also widely used for clearing and securing landing zones for Mi-8MTs tasked with delivering heliborne assault parties; the biggest assault operations in the early to mid-1980s often involved more than 60 helicopters.

The Mi-24V/P's Shturm-V anti-tank guided missiles were a commonly used weapon in such missions; this was renowned for its effectiveness in knocking out anti-aircraft artillery positions and machine guns housed in hardened shelters, while area saturation just before landing of the Mi-8T/MTs with assault parties was performed using S-5/S-8 rockets or cluster bombs. The main emphasis of Mi-24 strike operations involved a sudden fire attack and mutual support.

The combined bomb- and rocket-attack passes were performed with the rockets fired first, then hosing the target with machine gun or the 30mm cannon fire, then dropping bombs fitted with delayed-action fuses. Bombs proved to be particularly effective weapons in the mountains, whereas rockets fired at opposition strongholds had only a limited destructive effect. When helicopters were performing CAS missions, bombs could be used no closer to Soviet troops than 4,920ft (1,500m), and rocket and machine gun fire were to no closer than 1,640ft and 990ft (500m and 300m) respectively. For area suppression and action against personnel in the open RBK-250 cluster bombs were occasionally also employed.

While stationed in Afghanistan the 40th Army is reported to have sustained losses of at least ten per cent of its helicopter assets every year, which translates to between 30 and 40 machines during the worst years; half of these were Mi-24s. The helicopter attrition rate is said to have equated to one loss per 300–500 combat sorties. According to the authoritative Russian aviation magazine *Mir Aviatsii* ("World of Aviation"), no fewer than 122 Mi-24s were reported lost by Soviet Army Aviation in Afghanistan between 1979 and 1989. Annual losses of aircraft are distributed as follows: 1980, 21; 1981, five; 1982, nine; 1983, seven; 1984, 18; 1985, 21; 1986, 17; 1987, 21; 1988, three; 1989, three.

The average duration of sortie for the Mi-24 fleet was 60 minutes.

This view provides an idea of the typical rural environment in Afghanistan, where the Soviet Mi-24s were routinely required to strafe ground targets. (Alexander Mladenov archive)

In 1985, Mi-24s in theatre averaged 414 hours of flight each (the maximum utilisation accounted for 660 hours). The repair system used to return to service helicopters that sustained combat damage was constantly improved; in the latter half of the conflict the system was considered highly effective, as nine out of ten combat-damaged helicopters were promptly returned to the air.

In the first six months of 1987, when the FIM-92 Stinger and other shoulder-launched surface-to-air (SAM) types were widely used by the *mujahideen* (Afghan armed opposition fighters), the Soviet 40th Army reported at least 18 helicopter loses. The Jalalabad-based 335th OVAP reported the highest number of losses, with five of its helicopters shot down during this period. It is noteworthy that in one year of intense operations, between June 1986 and June 1987, the Mi-24-equipped squadron of 335th OVAP is reported to have suffered at least eight Mi-24s lost, and crewmembers killed on four occasions. One damaged Mi-24, which took a Stinger hit in the port engine in April 1987, is reported to have eventually managed to perform a safe emergency landing thanks to the prompt reaction of the pilot. The next day, this damaged *Hind* received a new engine and was subsequently ferried back to base, where it was repaired; not long after it resumed combat sorties.

The Afghan Air Force was also supplied with the Mi-24. Initially it received a number of second-hand *Hind-As*; later it received Mi-25s and Mi-35s which were also routinely used in operations against the armed opposition. Two Mi-25s were hijacked by their pilots and flown to Pakistan in 1985, and a few more defected to the *mujahideen*. A total of 36 Mi-24s were taken on strength by the Afghan government forces in the 1980s. After the Soviet Union withdrew from Afghanistan in February 1989, the Afghan Air Force *Hind* fleet continued to support government operations until the opposition seized power; then, the surviving *Hinds* were used in fighting between various factions of the new ruling coalition. After the Taliban seized power in Afghanistan in 1999, the only surviving Mi-24 was used by the Northern Alliance for occasional fire support missions, based in the Panjshir Valley.

A Soviet Mi-24 pilot wearing a lightweight summer combat outfit, including a ZSh-5 helmet and the NAZ-I survival vest; he is also carrying an AKS-74 submachine gun for self-defence. (Alexander Mladenov archive)

In combat around the world
Ethiopia
The Mi-24 received its baptism of fire in early 1978 in the so-called Ogaden war between Ethiopia and Somalia. The Ethiopian Mi-24As were used for close air support with great success, knocking out Somali armour and artillery. The *Hind-A* fleet was employed not long after to fight the insurgents in the breakaway territory of Eritrea. The huge *Hind-A* fleet, amounting to 40 machines, was used to strike at insurgent positions mainly employing the S-5 rockets used as an area-saturation weapon. No combat losses were reported although a few helicopters were burned out on the ground by Eritrean insurgents who raided Asmara airfield on the night of 21 May 1984.

In 1988 the Ethiopian *Hind* inventory was reinforced by a newly-delivered batch of Mi-35s (*Hind-Es*), which were immediately rushed into combat against the Eritrean separatist movement. In addition to destroying ground

Initially the S-5 57mm rocket fired in salvo was the main area weapon used by the *Hind*, but its lethality proved insufficient and in 1983 the S-5 began to be superseded by the much more powerful and far-reaching 80mm S-8 rocket. (Alexander Mladenov archive)

When performing close air support missions, bombs are allowed to be used at no closer than 4,920ft (1,500m) from one's own troops, while rockets (shown here exiting a 32-round 57mm launcher) and machine guns were limited to 1,640ft and 990ft (500m and 300m respectively).

targets, the Mi-35s were successfully employed against small boats in the Red Sea used by the insurgents for attacking commercial shipping. According to Russian sources, up to eight such vessels were destroyed in such attacks. It was also noted that the Mi-35s' UPK-23-250 gun pods were used with great success for attacks on armoured targets.

However, by the early 1990s the Ethiopian *Hind* fleet was in a very poor state due to discontinued support from the Soviet Union. Then in 1998 the fleet was revived thanks to the delivery of a number of new Mi-35s from Russia. These *Hind-Es* saw use in the later war with the newly-established state of Eritrea. Some information suggests that the helicopters were supplied to Ethiopia together with skilled mercenary pilots and technicians, and that they participated successfully in the brief but rather bloody war with Eritrea in 1998–99.

It is also noteworthy that the newly conceived Eritrean air arm was also supplied with a small number of second-hand Mi-24s from Eastern Europe which were used in the latter war. According to unofficial data, at least four Ethiopian Air Force *Hinds* were claimed lost during the war, although no information is yet available on any losses sustained by the Eritrean *Hind* fleet.

Vietnam

Vietnam was an early export customer, receiving the Mi-24A in 1980s. The Vietnamese People's Air Force rushed its *Hind-As* into action during the Vietnamese involvement in Cambodia, against the local Khmer Rouge insurgency movement hiding in the jungle. In the early to mid-2000s Vietnam still maintained a small number of its Mi-24As in airworthy condition, believed to be the last flying *Hind-As* in the world.

Iraq

The 1980–88 Iran–Iraq war was another early conflict that saw the *Hind* used in anger. At the beginning of the war the Iraqi Air Force had around

D The Soviet Air Force used its Mi-24 force intensively in Afghanistan, with at least 150 Mi-24s maintained there at any one time during the 1980s. After 1984, the *Hinds* operated under the constant threat of shoulder-launched SAMs already deployed, and the introduction of the FIM-92 Stinger system by the opposition forces in 1984 made things still worse. The Soviet reaction to widespread SAM employment by the *mujahideen* (Afghan rebels) involved improving the *Hinds* self-defence capability and changing tactics, switching to ultra-low or medium-altitude flying as well as avoiding zones with a known concentration of air-defence weapons. Mi-24 strike operations called for a sudden onslaught and mutual support, with combined bomb- and rocket-attack passes made, with rockets fired by the Mi-24P first, then the target hosed with the machine gun or 30mm cannon. When performing close air support missions, rocket and cannons were permitted to be used at no closer than 1,640ft and 990ft (500m and 300m) respectively.

The entire Iraqi Army Air Corps Mi-25 fleet remained on the ground during the 1991 Gulf War. At least three examples were reported as destroyed on the ground, with another captured intact by US troops at Basra. (US DoD/Staff-Sgt Dean Wagner)

40 Mi-24As and Mi-25s used predominantly in the classical CAS role, as well as for escorting assault transport helicopters delivering troops behind the front line. The Iraqi *Hinds* are also widely known for being involved in air-to-air engagements, mainly with Islamic Republic of Iran Air Force AH-1J SeaCobras and occasionally other helicopters and fixed-wing aircraft. There are conflicting accounts regarding the outcomes of helicopter-vs.-helicopter air combat; the Iraqi propaganda claims for an exchange ratio of 10:6 have been disputed by many Western war historians, and the same is true of the claim distributed by the Iraqi propaganda machine that a *Hind* even managed to shoot down an Iranian F-4D Phantom fighter near Aon Hoshah.

The Iraqi *Hinds* also saw much use in internal-security missions against the Kurdish separatist movement in northern Iraq in the 1980s, in which the Iraqi forces are known to have used chemical weapons; however, it is not confirmed whether the Mi-25s used such munitions.

The *Hinds* were also used during the Iraqi assault on Kuwait in August 1990, mainly to escort the Mi-8T and Mi-17 assault helicopters which delivered airborne troops tasked with seizing key locations. The Mi-25s suppressed pockets of resistance and knocked out armoured targets during the Iraqi attack on the capital city.

The Iraqi Army Air Corps' Mi-24As and Mi-25s saw considerable combat employment during the war with Iran in the 1980s, but were not used at all in the 1991 Gulf War. After the war the survivors of the Mi-24 fleet were used in internal security missions to suppress anti-government uprisings in the south and north of the country. (US DoD/Staff-Sgt Dean Wagner)

However, the entire Iraqi Mi-25 fleet remained on the ground during the 1991 Gulf War (Operation *Desert Storm*, January–March 1991); at least three examples were reported as destroyed on the ground and another one was captured intact by US troops at Basra. The Iraqi dictator Saddam Hussein continued to use the survivors of the *Hind* fleet in a bid to suppress rebellions in the north and south of the country after the end of the latter war.

During Operation *Enduring Freedom*, whereby a US-led coalition occupied Iraq in March 2003, the remainder of the once-powerful Iraqi Mi-24/Mi-25 fleet, deprived of support and spare parts during the long years of arms embargo, was no longer in airworthy condition and stayed on the ground during the advance of the coalition force.

Libya and Syria

As another early export operator of the *Hind*, the Libyan Air Force used its attack helicopter fleet in anger during the protracted operations in

Chad in the 1980s. The Mi-24As and Mi-25s supported operations of the pro-Libyan rebels there between 1980 and 1987. However, as a result of the Chad government forces' offensive in March 1987 three Libyan Mi-25s in good condition were captured at their base at Ouadi-Doum. These examples were handed over to France; one was retained there for testing, while the other two *Hind-Ds* were transferred to the US and UK respectively for testing

Libyan *Hinds* were frequently used in combat during the conflict in Chad in the 1980s. This is a newer Mi-35 *Hind-E* which is seen fresh from an overhaul in Ukraine with its machine gun removed. (Alexey Tirtov, via Alexander Mladenov)

and evaluation. At least five more Mi-24As and Mi-25s were lost in the conflict in Chad, being destroyed either on the ground or while in flight.

The Syrian Air Force's *Hind-D* fleet, delivered in the late 1970s, saw its first operational use in the 1982 war with Israel waged on the territory of Lebanon. The Syrian Mi-25s were rushed into combat to knock out Israeli armour, together with ATGM-armed SA342L Gazelle helicopters. The Mil types are reported to have amassed a total of 93 combat sorties and claimed as many as 55 armoured-target kills. No *Hind* losses were reported during the campaign.

During the following years the Syrian *Hinds* remained active in Lebanon, operating against the paramilitary Christian armed formations, and were also used in the coastal line blockade in areas controlled by the anti-Syrian militias. In April 1989 during one such patrol a pair of Syrian *Hinds* attacked by mistake two Soviet Navy support vessels, injuring seven sailors.

Africa

The Angolan Air Force was also among export Mi-24 operators which saw helicopters involved in extensive combat operations in the 1980s, against the UNITA opposition organisation, which received strong support from South Africa. Initially the Mi-25 version was used, while Angola received its first Mi-35s in the mid-1980s as attrition replacements. At least three Mi-35s were claimed as shot down by UNITA between 1988 and 1990. In 1987–88 the Angolan *Hinds* were used in the major battle against South African forces in the Cuito Cuanavale area. However, by the late 1990s the remains of the Mi-24 fleet were suffering badly from low serviceability due to discontinued support from the former Eastern Bloc. However, in the early 2000s the Angolan government renewed its operations against UNITA, using in combat a small number of Mi-35s restored to airworthy condition thanks to technical

Sudan's last batch of Mi-35s was delivered in 2005–6, and these *Hind-Es* are currently being used in the Darfur conflict in the western part of the country. (Rostvertol, via Alexander Mladenov)

support provided by Ukrainian and/or Belarusian contractors.

In Sierra Leone, a lone Mi-24V obtained second-hand from Belarus in the mid-1990s was initially flown by Belarusian and later on by South African mercenary pilots employed by the Executive Outcomes company. The Mi-24V flown by the combat-experienced South Africans was used to escort troop-carrying

Nigeria's few airworthy Mi-35Ps are involved in internal security missions over land and in the oil-rich offshore areas. (Rostvertol, via Alexander Mladenov)

Mi-17s as well as for occasional close air support missions mainly using 57mm rockets against the forces of the opposition Revolutionary United Front.

Nigeria is another African state where the Mi-35 has seen and is still used for counterinsurgency (COIN) missions. Similar missions are also regularly performed by the upgraded Algerian *Super Hinds* endowed with round-the-clock capabilities thanks to new equipment added as part of their upgrade by ATE of South Africa.

In Sudan, the *Hind* has been operating continually in combat since 1995, as the government waged war against the Sudanese People's Liberation Army (SPLA) in the southern part of the country, and in the Darfur region. In the 1990s at least two *Hinds* were lost in combat in Sudan. In 2001, the Sudanese *Hind* fleet was reinforced with up to 12 Mi-35s delivered from Russia, intended mainly to be used in the Darfur conflict. In 2007 one of these newly-delivered helicopters was downed by shoulder-launched SAM, and another was reportedly lost in action in Darfur in 2003. In 2005–6 another batch of *Hind-Es* was delivered to Sudan from Russia – up to 16 units – and at the time of writing the Sudanese *Hinds* continue to be used in anger within the country.

At the time of writing the *Hind* was still being used in the internal conflict in Chad that began at the end of 2007. In January 2008 the Chadian air arm's Mi-35s, flown by mercenary pilots from Eastern Europe were used in the COIN role against rebels based along the Sudanese border. The *Hinds* reportedly made numerous incursions into Sudanese territory in the Darfur area, to attack Chadian rebel groups seeking sanctuary in Sudan. On 18 January 2008, an Mi-35 flying a COIN sortie was claimed as shot down by the rebels; it is thought that if so, a Strela-3 or Igla shoulder-launched SAM was used.

In the 2000s *Hinds*, often manned by mercenary aircrews from the former Soviet Union, were actively used for fighting insurgencies in a plethora of other African countries, such as Uganda, Zaïre (Democratic Republic of the Congo), Congo-Brazzaville, Ivory Coast and Zimbabwe.

1. The Air Force of Zimbabwe took delivery of six *Hinds*, built at Rostvertol between 1998 and 2000. At least two of the helicopters are Mi-35Ps armed with the fixed 30mm gun. In 2000, the Mi-35Ps were upgraded by the manufacturer Rostvertol with the US-made Inframetrics IRTV 445MGII thermal imaging system usable for night-patrol missions. These *Hind-Fs* also feature NVG-compatible cockpits and their navigation system is enhanced with a Garmin 115L GPS receiver added to the DISS-15D Doppler sensor.

2. Russia's Internal Troops Service (Gendarmerie) of the Ministry of the Interior has integral air assets comprising a number of Mi-24 gunships. This service saw intense deployment in both the First and Second Chechen Wars (1994–96 and 1999–2000 respectively). The MoI helicopters can be easily distinguished from their Russian Air Force cousins by the vertical white strip on the tail boom.

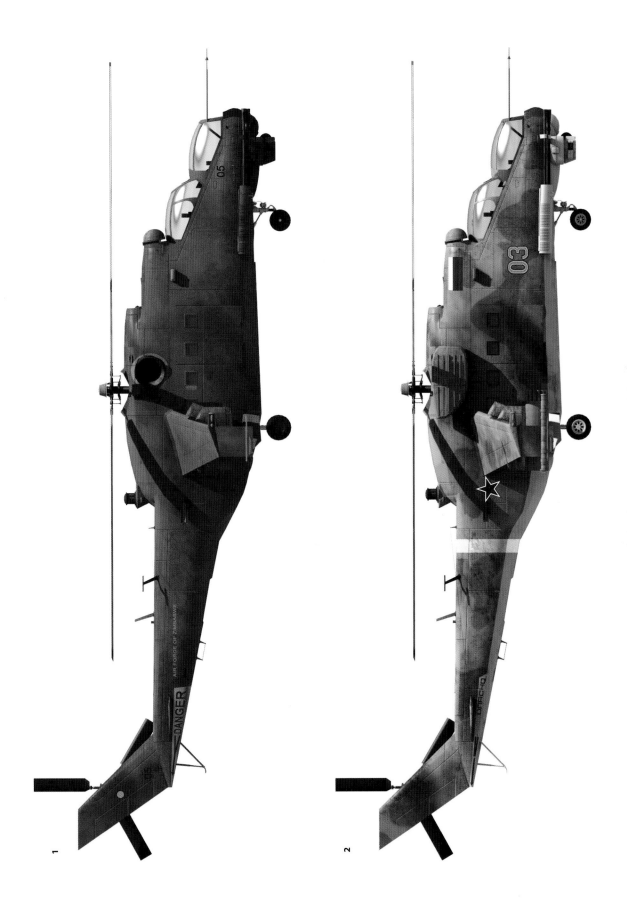

1

2

India and Sri Lanka

The Indian Air Force acquired its first Mi-35s in 1984 and these were actively used for the first time in 1987 during the conflict with Pakistan over the disputed territory of the Siachen Glacier. The Indian *Hinds* also saw active use in the COIN role in Sri Lanka while Indian peacekeeping forces were present there between 1987 and 1989. In the Sri Lankan conflict, the Mi-24Vs were used in operations against Liberation Tigers of Tamil Eelam (LTTE) insurgents, and employed rockets and machine guns. The Indian Mi-24 are also reported to have carried out numerous 'free-hunting' missions against boats ferrying weapons and supplies for the LTTE in the waters of the Palk Strait, separating India and Sri Lanka. No losses were reported in two years of operations. In the 2000s the Indian Air Force Mi-24 fleet was actively used in peacekeeping operations in Sierra Leone, mainly escorting troop-carrying Mi-8Ts.

The FYROM Air Force *Hinds* were intensively used in the counter-insurgency role in the summer of 2001, flying missions against positions held by ethnic-Albanian insurgents, set up in villages. (Alexander Mladenov)

The Sri Lankan Air Force became a *Hind* operator in 1995 and almost immediately rushed all six new aircraft into combat. The Mi-24Vs used against the LTTE sustained two losses to shoulder-launched SAMs and one more was damaged badly due to enemy action in 1987. In 1999, a further batch of six Mi-24s was taken on strength – a mixture of V and P versions procured second-hand from Ukraine. In the early 2000s, some if not all of the surviving Sri Lankan *Hinds* were upgraded by Elbit Systems with night-vision and self-defence aids in an effort to provide protection from shoulder-launched SAMs. The ElOp CoMPASS IV electro-optical payload, added as a part of the upgrade, was also employed as a target-marking device, using its laser-designating capabilities, to provide targeting for fighter-bombers dropping laser-guided bombs. The Sri Lankan *Hinds* were used in combat with notable success until the eventual defeat of the LTTE in 2009.

Latin America

The Latin American combat story of the *Hind* began in 1983–84 when a batch of Mi-25s was delivered to the Nicaraguan air arm for use by the pro-Soviet Sandinista government against the growing Contra insurgency movement supported by the US. At least two *Hind-Ds* were shot down by the Contras using Stinger shoulder-launched SAMs in 1987, while a third Mi-25 was hijacked to Honduras in December 1988. After the civil war's end in 1990 the *Hind* fleet was grounded due to lack of funds for maintenance; eventually the survivors of the Sandinista *Hind* fleet were sold to Peru.

The Peruvian air arm is another Latin American *Hind* operator, with 12 helicopters originally purchased in the early 1980s. These *Hind-Ds* were also used in anger over the years, participating in occasional COIN missions against the two principal insurgency movements in the country – the *Sendero Luminoso* ("Shining Path") and the Tupac Amaru Liberation Movement.

Croatia, Serbia and FYROM

Croatia was the only European Hind operator in the 1990s, using its Mi-24D/V fleet – hastily procured from Ukraine – in true battlefield offensive operations. Despite the UN arms embargo imposed in 1992, the Croatian Air Force managed to acquire a small fleet of around 12 Mi-24D and Vs in 1993–94. Some if not all of these *Hinds* were initially procured as unarmed armoured helicopters for medical evacuation, but soon after delivery were rearmed. The Croatian *Hinds* are said to have played an important role in the large-scale *Ulja* operation in 1995, regaining for Croatia the territory of East Slavonia, which had been occupied in 1991 by armed forces of the Croatian Serb minority. The Mi-24s armed with bombs and rockets operated from a number of forward locations close to the forward edge of the battle area.

In 1998–99, the Yugoslav Ministry of the Interior used a pair of Mi-24Vs, procured second-hand from Ukraine earlier in the decade in counter-insurgency operations in the breakaway province of Kosovo. After the end of the 1999 Kosovo war the Mi-24s were transferred to the Yugoslav Air Force.

The internal conflict in FYROM from 2001 is the most recent known combat use of the *Hind* in Europe. The first two FYROM Air Force Mi-24Vs, purchased second hand from Ukraine, were delivered on 23 March 2001, a few days after the outbreak of fighting between the FYROM government forces and the ethnic-Albanian rebels of the Kosovo Liberation Army (KLA) armed movement. The newly-delivered helicopters, crewed by mercenary pilots from former Soviet republics with rich combat experience, were rushed into action against the KLA in early April. The first combat sortie of the *Hind* in FYROM was flown against KLA positions north of the town of Tetovo on 2 April.

It is noteworthy that, as one pilot recalls, in two days of intense fighting in the summer the two Mi-24s managed to expend the entire reserve of 57mm rockets available in FYROM. The conflict also witnessed launches of more than 40 Shturm-V ATGMs, sometimes at night. The ATGMs were fired mainly against hardened KLA defensive positions established in stone houses in urban areas. During the siege of the village of Arachinovo, an Mi-24 was used with good effect to drop four 250kg bombs. The bombs were delivered just outside the KLA-held village, with the intention of intimidating the insurgents and weakening their will to continue fighting.

Until the autumn of 2001 eight Mi-24s were delivered from Ukraine, including two examples of the rare Mi-24K artillery spotter version stripped of mission equipment and used for CAS purposes only. In the spring and summer of 2001 only two mercenary aircrews (each comprising pilot and WSO) were used to fight KLA groups. The mercenary-flown *Hinds*

Russian Army Aviation Mi-24V/Ps saw active use in both the First and Second Chechen Wars, mainly being involved in close air-support missions. The main weapon used by the Russian *Hind* fleet in the first war was the Shturm-V missile, mainly for knocking out armoured targets and hardened defensive positions. (Mikhail Lavrov, via Alexander Mladenov)

in FYROM reportedly also amassed several night-combat sorties utilising US-supplied NVGs and receiving targeting from UAVs operated by the FYROM Ministry of the Interior.

The former Soviet republics

The Mi-24 played a notable role in the wars that followed the break-up of the Soviet Union in 1991. The first corner of the former Soviet empire to see the Mi-24 employed in combat was the Nagorno-Karabakh enclave in Azerbaijan; here, Soviet Army Aviation was initially used to patrol the skies over the areas where the warring factions (Armenian separatists and Azeri government forces) clashed. After Azerbaijan and Armenia eventually gained independence after Soviet dissolution, both countries inherited the Soviet Army Aviation units based on their territory. In the event, each country received 12 Mi-24s, and not long after both sides used their *Hinds* in anger. In 1992–93 Armenian forces claimed they managed to shoot down some four Azeri *Hinds* over the battlefields in Nagorno-Karabakh, while two Armenian Air Force helicopters were also reported as combat losses in 1992, shot down in the same area.

Civil war in another former Soviet republic, Georgia, also saw occasional use of the Mi-24. The Tskhinvali-based Soviet Army Aviation (later on Russian Army Aviation) regiment became involved in the conflict between Georgia and the breakaway region of South Ossetia. In June 1992 this regiment was disbanded and its helicopters transferred to Georgia. Only two months later these *Hinds*, this time bearing Georgian Air Force insignia, saw use against the militias in Abkhazia, another breakaway region of Georgia. At least two Mi-24s were shot down in the following battles, most likely by shoulder-launched SAMs fired by the Abkhaz militants. Russian Army Aviation Mi-24s were also used in the Abkhaz conflict, mainly for escorting ground convoys and transport helicopters into the combat zone.

In August 2008 the Georgian Air Force *Hinds* saw further much-publicised combat use, supporting ground troops in their ill-fated attempt to occupy South Ossetia. In this conflict the Georgian *Hinds* amassed a moderate number of low-level attack missions against militants and Russian forces in the South Ossetian capital of Tskhinvali using rockets and machine guns. No combat losses were reported in the course of these missions; only one machine crashed on its own territory, for reasons unknown, while another was destroyed on the ground by Russian airborne forces during a raid on Senaki airbase.

The Russian Army Mi-24s also saw considerable active service in conflicts in the former Soviet Central Asian republics. The first instance of combat

F The FYROM Air Force obtained six Mi-24Vs and two Mi-24Ks second-hand from Ukraine under a crash programme to procure heavy weapons for use in suppressing the ethnic-Albanian insurgency of the KLA armed movement. The first two *Hind-Es* were delivered on 23 March 2001, just a few days after the outbreak of fighting between FYROM government forces and the KLA. The newly-delivered *Hinds*, flown by very skilled contract crews, were rushed in action on 2 April. The Mi-24s, often operating in pairs, were used to attack KLA hardened positions in a number of villages. When destroying such small-size targets in urban or village environments, the Shturm-V missile was the *Hind-E's* weapon of preference, but for attacks on targets in the open S-5 rockets fired in salvo were the most commonly used weapon. The YakB 12.7mm machine gun also saw some use against soft targets. When performing low-altitude strafing passes to fire S-5 rockets or the flexible 12.7mm machine gun, the Mi-24Vs would always discharge flares as a precautionary measure against heat-seeking shoulder-launched SAMs that were believed to be in KLA hands.

Russian Ministry of the Interior Mi-24Ps and Vs were also used in combat during the conflicts in Chechnya, mainly for close air support of MoI internal troops (gendarmerie) during large-scale COIN operations. (Mikhail Lavrov, via Alexander Mladenov)

involving the Mi-24s occurred in Tajikistan, when the armed Islamist opposition there, supported by Afghan paramilitary formations, began a wide-scale drive to seize power in the republic in 1991. Russian forces stationed in Tajikistan and neighbouring Uzbekistan, supported by the Uzbek government forces, intervened promptly in a bid to suppress the uprising. In addition to Russian Army Aviation Mi-24s, *Hinds* belonging to the Uzbek and Tajik air arms were also used in combat against the Islamist opposition. One Russian Mi-24 was reported as lost in action on 18 December.

After defeating the main armed opposition forces in Tajikistan, combat shifted to the border areas with Afghanistan to involve Mi-24s belonging to the Russian Federal Border Guard Service, attacking Islamist bases on both sides of the border.

Chechnya

The first war in Chechnya was the largest challenge faced in the 1990s by the Russian Army Aviation. The first Mi-24 operations there were flown in November 1994, although a couple of months earlier Mi-24s with national insignia removed and supposedly flown by mercenary aircrews, were used to attack targets in Chechnya, supporting the pro-Russian opposition forces fighting against the ruling regime of Gen Dzhokhar Dudayev. The Russian Army Aviation Mi-24s, together with Su-25 close air-support jet aircraft were actively used to support the ground offensive against the Chechen capital of Grozny in November–December 1994.

The Mi-24s continued operating in Chechnya until a ceasefire was declared in August 1996. The war was considered unsuccessful for the poorly motivated and equipped Russian Army and Air Force which waged a poorly prepared and supported campaign. The motivation and morale of the helicopter crews was also low, so that the attack helicopters' effectiveness was questionable on many occasions. For instance, aircrews tried to fire weapons from as far away from the target as possible, using 80mm rockets and ATGMs, being unwilling to come within range of Chechen air-defence weapons, comprising mainly 23mm guns and a small number of shoulder-launched SAMs of various types. In addition, the majority of Russian *Hinds* used in this war were considered to be worn-out, experiencing numerous equipment and armament failures in flight. In 1994–95, as many as four Russian Army Aviation Mi-24s were reported lost in action during combat operations over Chechnya.

The second Chechen war, initiated in August 1999, was initially advertised as a large-scale anti-terrorist operation by the Russian armed forces. From the

Russia's Federal Security Service controls the Border Guard helicopter assets which comprise a large number of Mi-24 gunships. This Mi-24V, equipped with infrared suppressors on the engine jetpipes, is seen on approach at Khankala airfield in the troubled Russian republic of Chechnya in the early 2000s. (Mikhail Lavrov, via Alexander Mladenov)

outset it was primarily aimed at dislodging Chechen armed groups from fortified positions in the neighbouring autonomous republic of Dagestan, who had succeeded in occupying a number of towns and villages there with the intention of establishing control over this territory. During the 45 days of fighting in Dagestan, Russian Army Aviation was used intensively to support the push by ground troops and reported losses of two Mi-24s. Troops of the Ministry of the Interior also deployed their own Mi-24s for close air support of counter-insurgency operations and for escorting transport helicopters.

On 23 September 1999, on the eve of the rolling advance towards Grozny, Russian Army Aviation deployed in the region a total of 68 helicopters, 32 of them Mi-24P/Vs, to support the push into Chechnya of the Joint Group of Forces (JGF). Three groups of forces were established by the Russian Army – with a fourth added at a later stage – to undertake the occupation of Chechnya. Each group was supported by its own rotary-wing assets. The Eastern Group advancing from Dagestan had 12 helicopters, the Northern Group advancing from Russia had 16, and the Western Group advancing from Ingushetia had ten. Another 30 helicopters of various types were concentrated at the main Russian airfield at Mozdok in Russia, intended for use as reinforcements and operating under the direct control of JGF headquarters.

The large-scale offensive in what was considered to be Russia's "war on terrorism" was launched against Grozny from four directions simultaneously on 1 October 1999 and eventually led to the seizure of the city in January 2000. The high tempo of operations encompassing fire support, armed escort, medevac and utility missions, resulted in an astonishingly high rate of flying-time accumulation. From 23 September 1999 to 31 March 2000, a total of 7,233 hours were flown, with most aircrew logging between six and eight hours daily. The Mi-24V/P fleet operating in Chechnya is reported to have fired a total of 1,708 9M114 Shturm-V radio-command ATGMs between August 1999 and August 2000 (with only nine failures recorded), and together with the Mi-8MT/MTV fleet expended 85,269 S-8 80mm rockets and 89,850 rounds of 12.7mm, 23mm and 30mm ammunition.

Close air support for the advancing armoured spearheads was provided by so-called tactical aviation teams (TATs). Each TAT was composed of two to three Mi-8s and two to four Mi-24s which usually operated from forward refuelling/rearming

The Russian Air Force's upgraded Mi-24PNs saw their baptism of fire in 2005, flying combat missions in Chechnya. (Mikhail Lavrov, via Alexander Mladenov)

The most recent military conflict in which Russia was involved was in South Ossetia in August 2008. There, the Russian Air Force's upgraded Mi-24PNs were used mainly for daylight close air support operations, attacking the positions of Georgian troops advancing into South Ossetia. (Alexander Mladenov)

locations, situated in close proximity to the headquarters of the ground unit receiving aviation support. The TATs were often assigned to support the advance of motorised rifle regiments and usually operated in close cooperation with forward air controllers (FACs), located at the front edge of the battlefield area (FEBA).

During the initial stage of the campaign, so-called 'independent hunting' for targets of opportunity in certain kill boxes located deep within Chechnya was among the principal types of mission for the Russian Army helicopters. Such activity accounted for some 30 per cent of all combat sorties flown by the Mi-24s, in most cases, without receiving Mi-8 support. Targets attacked during these missions comprised weapons storage facilities, supply routes, makeshift petrol-processing plants, strongholds and horse/foot convoys entering Chechnya from the neighbouring state of Georgia.

The extremely high tempo of operations combined with mountainous terrain, inclement weather and last but not least the Chechen rebels' anti-aircraft fire, eventually took its toll on the Russian Army fleet. According to the Moscow military weekly *Nezavisimoye Voyennoye Obozrenie* ("Independent Military Review"), Russian Army Aviation recorded a total of 23 helicopter losses (11 Mi-24s and 12 Mi-8s) between April 1999 and August 2000, while 72 more helicopters sustained combat damage to various extents (all the helicopters had more than one instance of combat damage). Up to 23 damaged helicopters made forced landings and mobile repair teams

G

1. The Ethiopian Air Force was an early *Hind* operator, receiving its Mi-24As just in time to take part in the so-called Ogaden war between Ethiopia and Somalia in 1978. It was in this conflict that the *Hind* received its baptism of fire. The Ethiopian Mi-24A fleet, acquired second-hand from the Soviet Union and numbering some 40 aircraft, was used to knock out Somali armoured targets and provide close air support to ground troops. After this war, the *Hind-As* were involved in COIN operations against Eritrean separatists.

2. The Bulgarian Air Force received 38 Mi-24Ds between 1979 and 1985. At time of delivery the first few helicopters lacked Lipa IR jammers and ASO-2V chaff/flare-dispensers, but these systems were retrofitted later, while helicopters delivered after 1983 were factory-fitted with self-defence aids. The Mi-24s produced at the Rostov-on-Don plant (now known as Rostvertol) were initially painted in the standard Soviet Air Force two-tone camouflage scheme. Tactical markings included three-digit numbers applied to the engine cowlings. This example manufactured in 1985, wears a camouflage scheme applied in the early 1990s after overhaul at the TEREM-Letets facility in Sofia, Bulgaria. Up to six Bulgarian Mi-24Ds are earmarked for service-life extension in order to be usable beyond 2010.

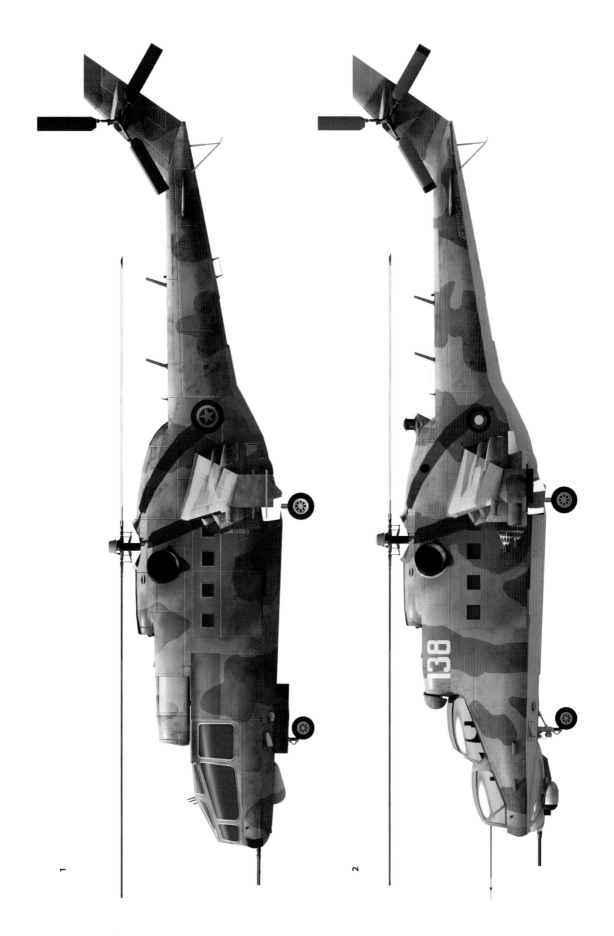

1

2

The Russian Air Force (Army Aviation branch) Mi-24s in Chechnya operated in pairs only, with the leader flying a 30mm gun-armed Mi-24P variant (seen here), the wingman usually an Mi-24V. (Sergey Soldatkin/Rostvertol, via Alexander Mladenov)

were used to fix 18 of these on-site while four others were recovered by Mi-26 heavy-lift helicopters.

In the initial stages of the Russian Army advance towards Grozny, the rebel's most dangerous air-defence weapons turned out to be a few ZU-23-2 twin-barrelled 23mm guns (truck-mounted in some cases) and a number of 12.7mm and 14.5mm heavy-calibre machine guns. However, the most commonly used such weapons were small-arms. Employment of shoulder-launched SAMs against RAA helicopters was recorded as late as August 2001. During the most intense days of clashes in Chechnya in 1999 and 2000, each day between six and eight helicopters sustained some kind of combat damage and up to four of these made forced landings. The main sources of such damage were 7.62mm and 5.45mm rounds fired from various Kalashnikov assault rifle and machine gun derivatives.

In the summer of 2000 when the second phase of the campaign began, the Russian Army Aviation had two composite helicopter squadrons with rotating air and ground crews, operating in support of the army units engaged in counter-insurgency operations in Chechnya; the rotorcraft were mainly tasked with troop/cargo transport and medevac. Other roles were to provide top-cover for ground convoys, 'free hunting' for targets of opportunity, and special forces insertion and extraction.

The Mi-24s of both squadrons operated in pairs only, with the leader flying a 30mm gun-armed Mi-24P variant and the wingman usually flew an Mi-24V. Over level ground the pairs flew mainly at ultra-low-level, while in mountainous areas they maintained an altitude of up to 1,000ft (300m), with spacing between aircraft of some 1,150–1,312ft (350–400m).

During the second phase of the campaign, the Mi-24s operated with an armament comprising two 20-round rocket packs for firing 80mm rockets and two to four 9M114 Shturm-V ATGMs, the latter used mainly to attack well-protected targets. When four ATGMs were carried, two were fitted with armour-piercing warheads for destroying hardened targets and the other two with thermobaric warheads – reportedly invaluable for neutralising enemy snipers hiding in buildings.

The S-8KO 80mm rocket fitted with shaped-charge/fragmentation warheads was the type used most frequently; the S-8D (DM) fitted with thermobaric warhead was employed on rare occasions. The Mi-24P's

The Mi-35M is the most advanced *Hind* derivative - a newly developed day/night-capable gunship with improved weapons suite and a host of performance-boosting airframe/powerplant/rotor system improvements. (Tina Shaposhnikova/Rostvertol, via Alexander Mladenov)

The *Hind* can employ a huge array of inexpensive unguided weapons, as shown here, and thus remains a pretty effective COIN and CAS platform. Second-hand examples originating in Russia and other East European countries are still frequently sold to Third World operators. (Alexander Mladenov)

GSh-30-2 twin-barrelled gun, usually provided with 150–200 rounds, was highly prized by *Hind* pilots thanks to its precision, lethality and high reliability. The YakB-12.7 four-barrelled machine gun had been considered demanding and prone to jamming, but also gained fame as a reliable piece of armament in the second Chechen war thanks to effective field maintenance.

The Mi-24s of the squadron based on Grozny North were also used to provide air escort of all military and paramilitary fixed-wing aircraft taking-off and landing at this airport. Performing this mission, the Mi-24s flew on both sides of the slowly-moving transport aircraft and used to pump flares until the protected asset had landed or gained a safe altitude, unreachable for shoulder-launched SAMs.

Mi-24 operators (past and present)

Abkhazia, Afghanistan, Algeria, Angola, Armenia, Azerbaijan, Belarus, Brazil, Bulgaria, Burkina Faso, Burundi, Cambodia, Chad, Congo-Brazzaville, Croatia, Cyprus, Czech Republic, Democratic Republic of Congo, Djibouti, Equatorial Guinea, Eritrea, Ethiopia, Germany (before that the German Democratic Republic), Georgia, Guinea, Hungary, India, Indonesia, Iraq, Ivory Coast, Kazakhstan, Kyrgyzstan, Liberia, Libya, Macedonia (FYROM), Mali, Mongolia, Mozambique, Namibia, Nicaragua, Nigeria, North Korea, Pakistan, Peru, Poland, Russia, Rwanda, Senegal, Serbia (before that Yugoslavia), Sierra Leone, Slovakia, Soviet Union, Sri Lanka, Sudan, Syria, Tajikistan, Tanzania, Turkmenistan, Uganda, Ukraine, United States, Uzbekistan, Venezuela, Vietnam, Yemen, Zimbabwe.

This unique category of battlefield helicopter firmly holds the title of most widely used fighting attack helicopter of all time, and is set to be known as such for a long time. (Mikhail Lavrov, via Alexander Mladenov)

INDEX

Numbers in **bold** refer to plates and illustrations.